JOHANNES BRAHMS

WALTZES
Op.39 (simplified version)
Edited by Howard Ferguson

INTRODUCTION

Johannes Brahms (1833-1897)

The *Waltzes*, Op.39, were composed in 1865 and published two years later in three versions: 1) the original, for piano duet; 2) for piano solo (difficult); and 3) for piano solo (simplified). Brahms himself made the two latter arrangements, sometimes altering keys for the player's convenience. The present text is based on the 1st edition of 3): *Walzer, Op.39 . . . leichte Ausgabe zu zwei Händen*; J. Rieter-Biedermann, Leipzig & Wintertür 1867. Pl. No.525.

Two other sets of waltzes by Brahms are the *Liebeslieder*, Op.52, and *Neue Liebeslieder*, Op.65. They are for solo vocal quartet (S.A.T.B.) and piano duet; but Brahms made arrangements of both for piano duet without voices, and of Op.52 for piano solo.

In this edition, Brahms' fingering is printed in italics and the editor's in upright type. A suggested metronome mark has been added within square brackets at the end of each piece. Though neither authoritative nor binding, it serves to show that different tempi are required to suit the strongly contrasted moods of the various waltzes.

HOWARD FERGUSON
Cambridge 1984

THE ASSOCIATED BOARD OF
THE ROYAL SCHOOLS OF MUSIC

WALTZES
Op.39
(Simplified Version)

BRAHMS
1865

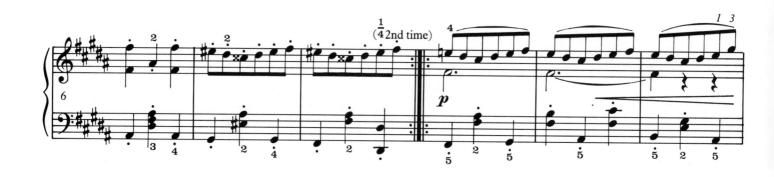

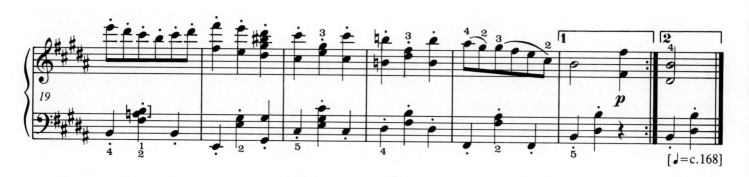

[♩=c.168]

A forthright curtain-raiser. In b.9 the *p* (subito) marks the change to r.h. *cantabile*. The *crescendos* that follow rise in two steps (first to b.12, then to b.16) to lead back to the *f* of the opening subject's return in b.17.

Brahms often used the word *dolce* to indicate a rather warm *cantabile*. In bb.10–11 the lowest l.h. line assumes momentary importance; and in b.15 the r.h. alto completes the expressive l.h. tenor of b.14. A slight *rit.* in bb.16–17 is followed by *a tempo* at b.18.

[♩=c.138]

Here the *dolce* is 'cooler' than in No.2, as befits the thinner texture. Some extra time is needed in bb.7–8 & 16–17, to allow the repeats to be negotiated smoothly.

Sostenuto in Brahms means 'slow'; so *Poco sostenuto* may here be taken as an indication that the *appassionato* is heavy rather than quick. Bb.15–16 may be slightly broadened; but bb.23–26 should, if anything, move on.

[♩=c.132]

Grazioso

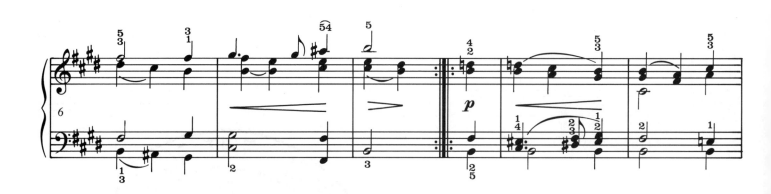

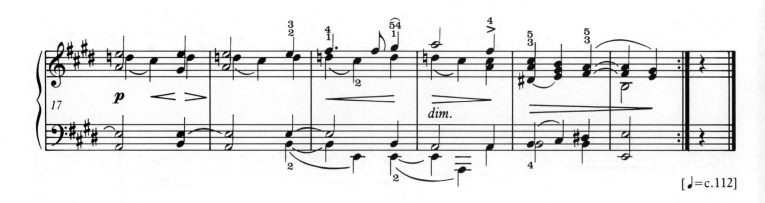

[♩=c.112]

The r.h. melodic line shifts from the lower part in bb.1–2 to the upper part on the up-beat to b.3–4. Likewise in the following four bars. In bb.16 &17 the 'hairpins' suggest a slight but expressive lengthening of beat 3.

In bb. 1–2, etc., think of the r.h. G–E, C–C & A–F as stretches rather than leaps, keeping the hand light and close to the keys. The little two-note arpeggios in bb. 3–4 etc., require a tiny flick of the wrist from left to right, in order to keep the upper notes stressed yet staccato.

One of the two slow Waltzes, and another example of *dolce* implying warm *cantabile* (cf. No.2) — at least in bb.1–9 & 22–37. The lighter-textured bb.10–15 are 'cooler'; but in b.16 there is an increase in dynamics to allow for the *dim.* (to *pp*) in bb.19–21. (The ⟩ in b.16 applies only to the l.h., as in bb.1–5.) Allow sufficient time to round-off b.21 before picking up the tempo in b.22.

[♩=c.96]

A gently lilting one-in-a-bar, with the single r.h. quavers much lighter than their neighbouring crotchets, the first of which should be slightly stressed in each bar.

Underline the *espressivo* by slightly stressing the first of each pair of slurred crotchets. On beat 1 of bb.17–22 & 25–27 the lower r.h.
note is stressed and the upper note *un*stressed in order to bring out the imitation between the two voices.

$[\ \flat =c.192]$

Keep the r.h. very supple for the *legato* 3rds in bb.1–4 etc., and make sure there is no break between the 4th & 5th quavers in bb.1 & 3.

(*a*) Gracenotes before the beat.

This Waltz has a strong Hungarian flavour that demands exaggerated contrasts. In b.9 there is a sudden drop from the dynamic level reached in the previous bar (say *mf*). In bb.15–16 the rests should be very pronounced, again *à la hongroise*. In bb.21–24 the lower r.h. line is most important. It needs a large *rit.* before the *fp a tempo* in b.25.

(a) Gracenotes before the beat.

[♩ = c.168]

An expressive stress is needed on the r.h. up-beat to bb.1–3, 14–19 & 22–24; it then shifts to the 1st beat on bb.5–6, 20 & 26–27. In b.25 an unmarked *p* should be added to beat 3, in order to allow for the *cresc.* two bars later.

[♩=c.120]

[♩=c.152]

Differentiate clearly between the heavy triplet upbeats, which are strictly in tempo, and the brilliant gracenote upbeats, which are as quick as possible. If the ornament in b.8 cannot be stretched as shown in the first interpretation of footnote (b), then the bracketed alternative will be found to give a very similar effect.

(a) Gracenotes before the beat.

Though the repeated notes in the l.h. could all be taken by the thumb, Brahms' fingering gives them a more incisive 'bite'. In bb.17–20 the prevailing *molto ritmico* relaxes into a *cantabile*, with syncopated r.h. stresses on the 2nd and 4th chords of each bar.

[♩=c.104]

If both upper and lower lines of the r.h. 6ths in bb.1–4, etc., are given equal prominence it provides a useful change of colour elsewhere, when the top line alone is *cantabile*. Bb.30–37 require some extra time, as they must on no account sound rushed.

(*a*) Gracenotes before the beat.

The final Waltz is slow, retrospective and autumnal. The counter-melody in the middle register is important. Be sure that the upper l.h. notes in bb.2, 4, 5 & 6 continue the r.h. phrase and are legato while the bass notes remain mezzo-staccato. In order to hear how it should sound, try playing the whole of the counter-melody in the r.h. *without* the upper part.

10/02

AB1868

Reproduced and printed by
Halstan & Co. Ltd., Amersham, Bucks., England